The Children Are Reading

Also by Gabriel Fried

Making the New Lamb Take

The Children Are Reading

Gabriel Fried

Four Way Books
Tribeca

Please direct all inquiries to:
Editorial Office
Four Way Books
POB 535, Village Station
New York, NY 10014
www.fourwaybooks.com

Library of Congress Cataloging-in-Publication Data

Names: Fried, Gabriel, 1974-, author.
Title: The children are reading / Gabriel Fried.
Description: New York, NY : Four Way Books, [2017]
Identifiers: LCCN 2017000672 | ISBN 9781935536949 (pbk. : alk. paper)
Classification: LCC PS3606.R54 A6 2017 | DDC 811/.6--dc23
LC record available at https://lccn.loc.gov/2017000672

This book is manufactured in the United States of America and printed on acid-free paper.

Four Way Books is a not-for-profit literary press. We are grateful for the assistance
we receive from individual donors, public arts agencies, and private foundations.

This publication is made possible with public funds from the New York State Council on the Arts,
a state agency.

We are a proud member of the Community of Literary Magazines and Presses.

Distributed by University Press of New England
One Court Street, Lebanon, NH 03766

for Archer and Nate, currently children

Contents

Where have the children gone this time?
There they are, behind the house,
standing in a cautious arc
around the flowers we warned them about.

I.

Ends Well

This is not the poem where the child comes back drowned.
He isn't pulled, unblinking, from the pond,
full of murky water as a janitor's sink.
Nor is it the poem where the child comes back maimed.
He isn't ruined by claws, teeth, gears, or fall
the way some children are we read about.

He wandered off while we were in a dream
or an argument. And, like something from a dream,
from a retold family story, the dogs went with him,
one on either side, as if suddenly called
to do something other than bask and forage.
So this is a happy poem, full of relief and just a little shame.

Maybe he only went to see the cows or followed
a dragonfly. Maybe he was enthralled by the carnage
of the barn, which twists like a ribcage in the field.
He's been walking now for longer than he hasn't.
He walked young: nine months, ten. It's always
seemed there's somewhere he is meant to be.

We've caught up to him at the greenhouse
and across the stream, past the silo and beyond
the air strip. He always comes back

willing, happy, even grateful; how can we scold him?
No wolf has seized him; he seems unchanged.
Nothing he's discovered has yet to matter.

Places Called Bogs

With all the naming taking up the space
on local maps (the gaps and the passes,
the swells and paths) you'd think that we'd have named
the bogs as well—that someone would have staked

a claim in honor of a family head
or kook. But I suppose a bog's no knoll,
no hollow—no *terra firma* into
which a stake will stick—nor is it truly

water, which seems to sing its name aloud.
There's something furtive in a bog,
some *sense* we sense we shouldn't name
or call attention to. And so we call

each bog *the bog*, and let that stand. *The mist
was rising off the bog*, we say. *The bog
is where they found that boy*; or *If you find
you've reached the bog, you've gone too far. Turn back.*

Potion

For dirt they use
the earth beneath
a fruit tree, mixed
with seeds and petals.

For sky they find
some blue inside
a wash bucket.

They add honey,
syrup of industry,
to ward off lies.
They stir in milk
for wholesomeness,
weeping as they do
so it convinces.

Instead of wine
they use the cherry juice
that's sat ten years
behind the licorice.

Then they let it stand
as long as they can.

They hold it to
the wind to hex it.
They hold it to
their lips to test it.

Twilight Field

The spirits play a children's game;
they pose as trees in clover.
I look. They stay. I look. They stay.
I look again. They're closer.

. . . until they reached a clearing in the middle
of the woods. There they stopped short.
Someone had been there not long before.
They could see footprints in the moss.
Whoever it was had walked to the center
of the clearing, but then had turned back,
as if he had found what he was looking for
or had forgotten something important.
Who could it have been? The prints
were too large for a cat, a rabbit,
or even a fox—and yet too shallow
for a wolf. They almost seemed made
by a small, barefoot man, though on closer
inspection they showed evidence of claws.
And they smelled faintly of rotten goat!

*

Amos stood naked in the parlor.
Whatever shall I do! he cried. It was too late
to return to town. Besides he couldn't go out
without his cap and scarf. And even if he could
find his clothes, his knees ached terribly.
What's more, something that felt like
quince jelly was matting down the fur

along the inside of his hind legs,
making it quite uncomfortable to walk.
It was beginning to attract bees.

*

Flora descended the passageway
for what seemed at least a quarter-hour.
How very long it is, she thought, *and how steep.*
The cottage appeared so dear from outside.

She continued onward. Several times,
she thought she heard footsteps.
But when she stopped to listen,
the footsteps ceased. And once,
a sudden draft, as if from a closing door,
almost blew out her lantern!

Flora found herself in some sort of storeroom.
In it were two enormous piles,
each one reaching nearly to the ceiling.
One pile was of almonds.
The other was of a fruit she'd never seen.
Its peel was crimson and its perfume

was like mead, pleasant but quite insistent.
Flora suddenly felt rather faint from hunger.

*

He stood above the brook and gazed sadly
at his reflection. His jacket was stained
from the port, and his fine, new waistcoat
was torn from all the fawning.
Three young trout poked their heads through
the waterline just where his face reflected
back at him. They mocked him, singing
Oliver Ermine, used to looking so fine
Oliver Ermine, used to looking so fine.
Then they spouted water all over
his handsome pair of nubucks.
He never could get the water stains out.

*

She went around to the far side of the cottage
wearing work gloves and carrying a basket
woven from cattails. There she collected
an alarming assortment of growths and vegetation,
including rhubarb leaves, nightshade, and foxgloves.

She stopped to collect a discarded peach pit
from the rubbish heap, before going to the tool shed
in search of a mallet. When she returned to the kitchen,
the broth on the stove had begun to simmer.

*

And that was the last that anyone ever saw
of Doctor Julian Jackal.

The Children Are Reading

They disappear from broad daylight,
like shadows midday that stay
away mysteriously as afternoon
extends westward, further from town;
and the swings that seemed to swing
from recent play are just a thing
the limp of August breeze can lean on.

In that disquieting climate,
which comes when regular silence
is silent too long, they are tucked
within a crumbling shed,
a rusted-out truck,
or the magical hollow
of an impenetrable thicket.

There, in the stable of their own
kidnapping, they are reading.

They are reading their own story
again and again, in book after book—
the one of a girl looking after a boy
in rail yards, burned-out churches,
and the forest's bad neighborhoods.

The girl reads each one first, before
passing it on, sometimes holding
the book once he's grasped it, as if
to say *I shouldn't let you*

hurt the way this one will hurt you.
But she does, and it does hurt him.
Often she watches him read what

she's read, hours with those same pages.
Then, when he's raised his thick eyes
to hers, they bow their heads together
and speak sparingly—their vow
not of silence but magnitude.

They scrape *I love you Charles Wallace*
in the earth with a stick while she
explains his hurt to him in words
unspoken in town, in the houses
that are scattered like handfuls
of acorns around the county.

And once the sun has bled out
down the mountain, the air turned to silt,
and they have made their ways home

through the trees (one to silence, the other
to the hot scold of fermented breath),
they lie awake in bed, full of newfound
endlessness, imprinted as paper
from a typewriter's necessary violence.

Orphans

"Let's play orphan! Our parents are dead!
Dad was sick in the heart, Mom in the head!
We'll hide in the cellar, no one will find us
behind the broken flowerpots and mattress.
You bring waffles, I'll bring a lighter."

Summer Stock

In June, the children stage a play of their own making,
their roles a weird assortment of future and past
lives: landlord, hypnotist, postmaster, pioneer,
forest ranger, reporter, and mother superior.

At dusk they rig a shower curtain to the clothesline
running from our house to the shed nearby.
Like us, they know to use the sunset as a spot,
as if they've been performing since before they could walk.

Their play's an eerie thing; it's full of unintended truths
that border on fact—of misconceptions that ring true.
When the landlord says with a laugh he's used
the hypnotist to disgrace the nun, some of us gasp.

Will the reporter, undercover, expose all?
Will the postmaster release the confiscated package?
The curtain closes at the end of the act, and we sit dutifully
beneath the moon, eager for resolution,

but the children don't come back.

The Little God

The little god emerges from behind the shed
in his red leotard and his cowboy hat.
He doesn't always show up when we pray,
but mostly he humors us, strutting out belly first.

The little god is not my son disguised as a little god;
it is the other way around, it turns out.
I have a son, an older one; you would have thought
that I would know the difference. Now it is too much

to think of if the god was ever my son—
of whether he has been replaced
by a little god identical to him
or whether he was never mine, exactly.

Maybe it's the same, the not-knowing
and the not-thinking of not-knowing.
Maybe, even if he were my son,
I would feel this same uneasy reverence.

Lizard Queen

North of town, a castle undeterred by time or place.
Along its porticos between the turrets in the summer blaze,

she walks its perimeter, shadow to light, light to shadow.
Her footsteps are a sibilance of naked soles on stone.

Between her legs, the geckos scurry to and fro. Their tails flick
her feet where the friction starts to tear the skin.

She is larger than their life—than anything cold-blooded.
Her hair's let loose where the castle wall plummets

to slide through the fists of those who dare try climbing.
She is coax and she is antidote. She is lingual and slither.

She is edged yet curved as wind engorging a sail.
She is a model that was never drawn to scale.

Kumari

I was perfect when they came, all twenty
of my teeth aligned like stars within me.
They held a conch beside my ear to see
how I was made. They handled me gently.

Where I found composure not to cower
or cry out, only the goddess can say.
I am the goddess at least one more day.
You may question me, but I won't answer.

If it's an *answer* you need—or *wisdom*—
ask it of men. I am daunted by these
human things. *Serenity. Balance. Peace.*
They are words (worse, terms) for what seems wordless.

But press your head to my sole. I'll let you
feel the swell I've heard my body conveys,
as cool and hairless as a holy clay.
The goddess gives you power to be soothed.

Do it soon, though, while it's still mine to give:
It's many years now I have been a girl.
One day, like a whip, the goddess will uncurl.
Then blood will run from me, and I will live.

The Drawing

Not only could a child make this art, one did.
And now we're fixed before it like a copse

before a coming storm, rooted in place,
unable to turn away until the winds

twist us from ourselves, riddling us
with rocks and loam, a force of nature

that we claim to love but come to fear,
a portrait that we cannot stand to face.

On Lewis Carroll's Final Photograph of Alice Liddell (1870)

By now, having been made larger than life,
her skin just will not sit right anymore.
It's not that it has stretched out as she's grown
(and shrunk)—elastic gone, thin as playing
cards—but she's fallen to a shape inside
it, like shifting in a costume that fits
askew, eyes slipping over her eyes,
its edges jabbing her between the ribs.

She's forced to turn away—in insolence,
it seems, slumping from his lens, his bulbous
pen. (The things that turned her first from girl
to girl. She's woman now; no lens hides that.)
Though what is insolence but wordlessness,
defense against the versions of ourselves
we do not author, sewn or realized
for us in our muted presence, made
in our absence: of a disappearance.

This not Alice posed in beggar rags
or picnic finery who peers out from
a separate skin. From her retreat
within, who knows, really, where she's wandered.

The Roly-Poly Pudding

O dough ball, O child.
Here I find you: gagged,
sooty, bound with strings
from a toy guitar.

I know I say
there are no monsters,
that we are safe,
as safe as houses,

but no one ever knows
what creeps the attic,
flue, or crawl space
once we break from day,
when the door is shut,
when the cat's away.

The Story of the Castle Robbers

Tonight my father tells
the story of the castle,
how after the big earthquake

two men—"one an art professor,
the other a smuggler
of stolen art—creep into

the crumbled turret of
Etruscan stones to pick the castle
of its prizes." (He always uses those

same words; I say them with him
softly; my brother always shouts
"*I* AM A SMUGGLER!")

The men move through the rubble
and the shadows of the rubble
that their flashlights cast

along the floor. Each room is bigger
than our house, my father says.
The noise those men make echoes

in a way that's loud enough
to get them caught, but small.
The smuggler's like a fox;

the professor knows more
about painting than creeping.
Besides, the castle won't keep quiet:

it makes music from their steps
and breathing, music I worry
might wake up something secret.

When the men reach the library
of special books and maps,
and also seven special chairs,

my brother shouts, "Embarrassment
of riches!" like he's learned to
(and like I refuse to).

The men fill their truck, but there's more
than they can haul, so they decide
to come back once the coast is clear.

I don't know everything, not yet,
but I would never come back.
And even though I know this story,

I bunch the sheets up in my fists
the way I do when Rikki-Tikki goes
to get Nagina's eggs out in the garden.

But nothing happens to the men
the second time, except one thing:
they find there's still too much

for them to take. And so they come
another time, after the police
have given up on finding them.

My brother always shouts for more
of everything (more snacks, more
time, more *more*), but I have learned

that it feels strong to want something,
to keep the wanting for myself
instead of asking to be filled.

The men are caught that third time.
Everyone knows that, even if you've
never heard the story. And now

my brother's shouting from the stairs,
who knows what for, and the dark
outside our window's full of quiet.

School-Night out in a Venn Diagram

We stand in the sliver
of shadows the circles
from streetlights make.
We are almost out
too far, in a space
barely safe and daring;
ensphered in night,
its creature comforts,
a darker shade of night
around it.

Escort

I am small and have never been a threat.
We walk, the two of us, through the forest.

We come upon a figure, or—though still,
back to a fir—it comes upon us,

the sudden sunset having made us
blinder even than we've been.

Who's this? the figure says to me.
Your sister? You have a beautiful sister.

Outside Over There

We find the book left open by the stairs—
salted and wet—no children anywhere.

Note Left on the Counter after a Science Fair

Gone to hunt
for metalmarks
and milk quartz.
Home eight minutes
after last light
leaves the sun. Look
for fireflies—we have
orange peel, book
of matches.

The Story

After I returned, forewarned,
from the storyteller's home,
I lay in bed on my side, like a patient:
knees bent, back to the room.

The story had slid inside me;
I could feel its ends
(who can tell head from tail?)
latched against me, hooked

to my anus and nostrils, so that
when I moved or even thought
of moving it pulled me
to myself, opening me

to every intensity.
Before long it had deployed
a tendril up around my spine,
and every neural fascicle sang

like a hive, an ancient chorus,
thrumming in astonishment
as the story whispered, licked lips
to my inner ear, its perpetual disclosure.

Colony Collapse Disorder

At first it was as morals sung
in passed-down workaday rounds:
a few of us didn't return so
a few of us went searching.

And at first it didn't matter
or even measure, the thrum
of the hive no different, a pulsing
glove with fingers extended.

What is five or fifty?
Like rain drops in a storm
from an endless cloudbank.
Like drips from honeyed plunder.

But when the poets gathered
(first one, then four, scratching),
we wondered; we wondered
we wondered. Now I wander.

Abecedary

Apple-
Bodied
Child,
Debonair
Elf,
Forage
Gently
Here
In
Jasmine-
Keeled
Latitudes.
Mighty
Newish
Otter,
Pray
Quietly.
Retrieve
Sapphires.
Trundle
Under
Violets
Within
Xanadu,
Young
Zodiac.

Stutter

It's not the question he delays as his
small engine over-revs in loops and stammers.
It's not the question—the question
is clear. It's the answer.

Scold

"You treat imagination like dammed water,
letting out a little at a time, hoping it will
generate the proper sort of
energy. It would be

one thing if you stood
on top of the dam and let the dizziness
take over, the high
water and the low water

doing their real work, forcing
a stretch you really felt
in your groin. But
you stand on the riverbank

and watch it like it's doing tricks
for you, and even struggle
from there. Either come up
here or let the water

out in one burst! You think
it will sound wrong,
that it will hurt.
Maybe it will, how could I know?

I'm a child. You think
that I'm a metaphor, that you can
learn something from me.
I hear you tell your friends

about me, even though I can't
possibly be listening.
You think I am lost in my own world.
Well, I am and I amn't.

I'm a dam myself, with no idea
of what's on either side.
I just lie back, sense
the potential, and see stars."

The Field

If you sit in a field for long enough
the field becomes you.
Swallows circle your neck,
a fox reverses through you like a dream.
An owl takes your young,
your young are rabbits, their taking fate.

The trees eventually drop their guard,
they drop their leaves to earth.
But first the nights and days of bats and sheep
propel the summer.
Squirrels skirt then perch upon you,
their bites into your shoulder tentative
then deep, sustaining, blood
descending their chins.
A caravan appears in time,
immigrants or actors, a boy
on a camel, no it must be a horse,
you wave or shoo them,
they cannot tell, they are far as can be,
their route won't intersect
with the stump you've chosen.

If you sit in a field for long enough,
you are always in that field
no matter where you wander.
You are always in that field,
and not just sitting. You rise
sometimes and dance,
throwing yourself with a grace
belying each of your obstacles
(the body, the self-conscious spirit).
And no matter where you are
when you dance this way,
the field explodes with something—
a swarm, kaleidoscope, or blossom.
And you venture on like this, you and the field,
whatever light or storm befalls you.

These gods are crude and crudely drawn
as if to show the timelessness
of their rendering: childish
in manner, throwing their tantrums
the way we might have thrown a rock
in anger from atop a hill,
even the roof, when older—
old enough to know what we might
break, brute enough to cause damage
it would take a god to undo.

The Cadmean Vixen

After she's certain the gods are dead
(or in whatever deadened state is dead

for gods) she breaks the stony pose
she's held a thousand years or more,

twitching an ear and flickering her whiskers,
before trotting off in search of boys or chickens.

Pan

And now where have they been, the boys?
Something's missing from their eyes,
something trusting, something kind
cast off like skin or old toys.

The farm that reeks of shit in summer—
they smell of it, their breath so thick
we gag. Could they have traveled
all that way while we were staring,

returning to us feral, with a blank mistrust
that borders on intent to kill?
They've become the rivals we forgot we had,
—their nails clotted with muck and rust—

untended, cloven, aroused.

The Joy of Sex

Too high to reach
without a chair
but low enough
to read the spine
and wonder, down
against the bed skirts
and the shag rug.

Late Winter after Art Class Papier Mâché

Outdoors a dungeon of sludge:
March snow, March mud. Beneath us
we lug our legs homeward,
the weight of the day
still on our hands.

Mrs. Hortense Honeybee was beside herself.
She could not budge
no matter how she tried.

She would fall behind
with the pollen, she just knew it!
The entire village would be buzzing
about having to settle for jelly
instead of honey.

Why had she ever agreed
to let in Cousin Imperia?
Wasps were always such unpleasant guests.
But Hortense could never say no
to family; it would be her undoing!
Already Imperia had offended
the neighbors with her droning.
And now she had paralyzed Hortense
and injected larvae into her abdomen!

*

Gallus Cockadoodle stood before the mirror
in the trailer in a corset stuffed with duck feathers.
He had forgotten the trauma of his abduction;
indeed, the ache in his ribs was almost pleasurable.

He knew he should be planning his escape
but instead could only think of how pleased
his captors would be with his outfit;
the garters made even his paltry legs enticing,
and the pasties on his wattle and comb danced
in the lamplight like stoked embers when he shook.

*

Whatever could have made such a mess
and such a stench!
Mister Pishy-Poshy couldn't imagine!
Nor could he have conceived of such decadence—
the wadding and smearing, unspeakable
applications of gardening implements.
No English creature could
possibly be responsible.
It must have been a Scot,
perhaps someone from the Continent!—
or more likely, the Colonies—
an Australian or an American.

The Amateur Magician

I wave a wand of scant magnetism
above a plastic cup,

willing a little vanishing:
the correct commotion.

With each attempt, I disappear
within my visible body,

while elsewhere, in the grass
in a factory, after endless

searching, a boy finds his watch,
a ball, elucidation, joy.

II.

The Butcher

A hamlet like this one, barely
half a mile of a two-lane
state road rolling through the farmlands,
doesn't always have a butcher.
This one does. There is a butcher
but there aren't any doctors.
There is a dentist but no gas
station. The nearest grocery
store with aisles is half an hour,
a little too far in summer.

The butcher works from his sisters'
shop of canned goods, milk, the local
paper. He's not old, but he is
too old to live with his sisters
for no reason. They're unmarried,
though, childless; he's the baby.
Maybe they need him somehow,
the four of them in cardigans
identical to boys looking
to buy gum without pats and praise.

The butcher is a giving man.
In fall, when Jamaican migrants
work the orchards, he slaughters goats

they roast on spits just down the hill
from church, though it makes him nervous.
In winter, when the Anglicans
in Milton Turnpike have no meat
to sell in their shop, he sells them
chops at cost, butcher to butcher,
saying nothing to his sisters.

And in spring, because the Jewess
from Boston has mentioned her love
of morels, he hunches over
the underbrush of half-formed trails.
Often he is in his apron, smudged
with blood, having stolen away
at lunch with a wicker basket.
He rustles out the risky things,
which often crumble in his hands,
the muscles a butcher can't help

but have impeding his secret,
lonely love affair with longing.
Searching, he lets himself think
of the Jewess's perfect flank.
Her tenderloin. Her bottom round.
He blushes helplessly at his

bad jokes, then pushes through the shame
of being grown up and merely
well liked, and returns to her curves.
He's sure she'd never think of him

as crude, but as a man
who adores her and cannot help
who he is or how he will fail her,
crouched on paths in woods between
the dark and holy spears of light.
She's almost entirely his
creation. Yet she could well be
as real as this, smelling of good
dirt like the mushrooms, those shy blooms
of the private earth he searches for.

The Poet

Gardiner, Maine

We figured him a monk or a pervert,
the way he simply stared out from his porch
each afternoon. He seemed too young to be
either, a baby face hidden beneath
his moustache. At the same time, he was broad
and strong as lumber; that's what it looked like,
anyway, when he stood up from his stool at the bar.
I'd watch him there sometimes; he'd come at eight,
leave by ten. Sometimes his jaw would tremor,
about to join in, maybe, but too late
always, by the time he summoned courage.

It's not that he seemed dangerous to us
(though how could we have ever really known)
but rather that he fell between the clear
divides of danger and safety: quiet
always feels that way—in the mill, the woods.
It sets the stage for God knows what surprise.
A floor giving in, rifle fire.

He came and left a dozen times before
he left for good one spring when the ice
gave way, the Kennebec exploding
toward the ocean. He was like a truck been
stuck in a ditch, rocking to free itself.

He never came back, though we heard
of him, of course. Never minded what he
wrote—liked it, even—and some are just made
for Away. Others never forgave him, though,
for spending those summers in New Hampshire.

Alice Meets Peter

on the Meeting of Alice Liddell (Lewis Carroll's Alice), 80, and Peter
Llewelyn Davies (J. M. Barrie's Peter Pan), 35, in London, 1932

She has shrunk for good by now,
and he's grown up in spite of everything:
a publisher, of all things, a maker of books.
They've never been the stories of themselves;
no one is, but these two least of all. Who escapes
the fetishes of childhood that others make?
The outfits and mispronunciations are hard enough
to shake; the tantrums and unintended wisdom;
the resistance for no good reason to rain
boots or parsley. But their two stories stick
to them like shadows, never gone long.
Even this encounter will be legend,
stagy as it is, this meeting of these two old children always
played by girls, who some say never were
      whom some think they ever are.

Landscape with Model Trains

He makes a little
world within
the little world
beneath the sky-
light in the attic,
baggage blue
with Pan-Am
labels stacked
against a wall,
his silent Purple
Heart inside
a shoebox.

Sheep's Clothing

It was my son who saw him first up there—
no. No, it was the dog. My son heard her
begin her silent whine, and so he looked
where I no longer look when the dog whines.

What he saw was a boy up on the hill,
the hill beyond the wall beyond the field,
so *far*, in other words. I had to squint
to make him out. For sure it was a boy,

though, the way he stood there, his shoulders slack.
Not a boy the way my son is a boy,
the kind who still shuffles in each morning
to climb into bed with the dog and me.

The boy up there was the height of a man,
and not a short one, against the pink sky.
It wasn't right to see him standing up there.
It was a winter afternoon and cold

and for all I knew, he was underdressed
and his hair was wet. The sun was sinking,
and I couldn't think of a boy his shape
who lived in this town or the town over.

But there was something else that wasn't right,
the way we three all knew to stay indoors
just then, without even a word or growl.
We three kind souls, who are always hungry

for connection, who flock to it like birds
to suet, knew to hunker down and wait
out night's erasure, together in darkness
until our one breath was thick with sleep.

The Night the Train Bridge Burned

That night the river was a bale of flame,
the burning tracks, two hundred feet above,
reflecting for miles to the north and south.
Some say the glow reached ten counties,

growing like a rumor with the tide
until the whole valley was full of it.
The woods on each steep bank rustled
with a horse's fire-panic in the fan

of heat, the black sky imperceptible
beyond the sudden, local, stellar light.
Wherever we stood to watch was marooned
in time: hilltops and fire escapes, the park

we skate in when the freeze is deep enough
in winter. Never mind the other bridges,
decades old and built for cars. Never mind
the one-gate airport across town, dispatching

DC-9s to Plattsburgh, Rochester, even Boston.
Never mind the progress soon to come,
two years off or twenty, prototypes
overheating outside Tokyo and Berkeley.

That bridge was the span to before our time.
Trains deposited generations of New England
college boys between the thighs of Vassar girls.
They carried us to grandparents shuffling

through the summers in the Catskills, to aunts
moved on to Cooperstown and Scranton.
They journeyed through our nights, miners
disappearing beneath a mountain, ever hopeful

of tunneling through, of making thoroughfares
for light. How, now, will we find our American
way westward? How will our small son
cross the river's new expanse? How will we

navigate our own insistent yearnings, familiar
though they be, now that they float beyond us
like ships adrift on an uncharted ocean,
                    night after starless night?

Dawn

He drives his son, now ten, beyond the town
to show him where he was a boy himself—
to see the bog thick bubbles surfaced from,
the stream that carried ships the size of cats
they made of Styrofoam and tin foil.
Here is the tree they disappeared inside:
its branches wrapped them like an owl's wings;
and over here, their first erotica,
the clothesline where the neighbor hung her bras.

And here's where they broke bottles on the rocks,
and past that ridge is where they did the things
to kittens—one time, and not all of them.
Here's where the man approached him: here and there.
And there's where the river took him under;
there is where it let gasp for air again.
Here's where his faith betrayed him when the floor
gave way; here's where the ghost thrust in its blade.
Here are thorns, temper; there is nightmare, cave.

And over there's the wild flower field.
And there's the tree a god made of a girl.
There are evergreens, and there Rome Beauties.
There's the shrine, the monolith, the temple.
There's the fire pit; there's the city's glow.

And there's the road that took him far away.
There it is again—the one that brought them.
There's the sunset, barely worth describing,
its pageantry so wild. And here's the dawn.

Vespers

At six tonight, the church calls out to God,
like a girl who sings at chores
and doesn't know her voice cascades
down hills, through groves, and into homes.

It is not Sunday, or even midwinter
when the soul believes itself to be hungriest;
the lot beside the church is empty,
which doesn't mean the church is—

the town is small and close,
the air is fine. It *is* almost empty, though:
just a few widows stoop in the pews
beneath the dusty slats of late-day sun.

The boys who stalk the graves nearby
have never been inside to pray.
Neither has the new shopkeeper
(from India, it's assumed, though maybe not

the Christian parts) nor the man who owns
the orchard on the Oxford–Lloyd town line.
(It's said the fruit grows better in the town
with fewer debtors listed in the *Herald* each April.)

The florist only comes for funerals, his tie
matching the arrangements; others seek solace
elsewhere: ravines, the dive by the truck-stop.
For some months, a schoolteacher—a Czech

whose surname only her students can spell—
slips in and out, almost undetectable.
She is gone now, though: married and moved
away, or moved away and married.

But if the church is empty, its long chimes
fill the town with prayer: a prayer for continuing
stillness, a prayer for an empty womb,
a prayer for music meaning something

more than song. And if the age of congregation
ended awkwardly (the same caution told
a third time to the same gracious crowd),
the valley still feels full of private worship.

It may come out of something less than piety:
Superstition. Shame. The scoffed-at hurt
that people nowadays call Nostalgia,
embarrassed at being moved by something

holding its ground, sturdy as seasons. We're sure
for all the world the church is only wood,
some nails, a coat of paint the pastor himself
slaps on each June, sweating like a layman;

yet here we are in its proximity—in yards,
on porches, walking tractor ruts,
rolling Pontiacs down South Street,
windows wide open, letting its chiming in.

Our backs may be to it, our eyes focused
on the holes we dig with some sort of spade.
It's true, these days we're warier than we were.
But still it is evening, and we still pray.

Notes

In "The Children Are Reading," the phrase "I love you Charles Wallace" comes from an essential moment in *A Wrinkle in Time* by Madeleine L'Engle. This poem is for Amanda Touchton.

"The Lizard Queen" is for Monica Ferrell.

A kumari ("Kumari") is a prepubescent Nepalese girl, believed by certain Hindus and Buddhists to be the living incarnation of the goddess Durga. She is removed from her family and worshipped until she menstruates, at which point she is no longer considered divine.

"*The Roly-Poly Pudding*" and "*Outside Over There*" are responses to eponymous children's books by Beatrix Potter and Maurice Sendak, respectively.

"The Field" is based on *Mesocosm*, a 146-hour animation cycle by Marina Zurkow, which can be viewed at www.o-matic.com.

"The Cadmean Vixen" refers to a giant fox of Classical mythology that can never be caught, sent by angered gods to eat the children of Thebes. Tasked with defeating the fox, the general Amphitryon summoned Laelaps, a magical dog from which no prey could escape. To solve the paradox of an inescapable dog hunting an uncatchable fox, Zeus turned both animals into stone and cast them into the night sky.

"The Amateur Magician" is for Lisa Russ Spaar, a professional magician.

"The Poet" is inspired by E. A. Robinson.

"Landscape with Model Trains" is in memory of my grandfather, Nathan Rosen.

"The Night the Train Bridge Burned" is based on a May 8, 1974 fire on the Poughkeepsie (New York) Train Bridge. This poem is for Jared Finkselstein.

Acknowledgments

Thanks to the editors of the following publications, in which poems included in this book were originally published, sometimes in earlier versions or with different titles: *32 Poems, American Poetry Review, Catch Up, The Chronicle of Higher Education Review, Cellpoems, Green Mountains Review, Guernica, Kenyon Review, The Literary Review, Memorious, Subtropics, Traveltainted,* and *Yale Review.*

Thanks, too, to the Civitella Ranieri Foundation and the MacDowell Colony for indispensible residencies, and to the Department of English at the University of Missouri for defraying travel expenses to and from these residencies.

My gratitude to Martha Rhodes, Ryan Murphy, Sally Ball, Bridget Bell, Clarissa Long, and others at Four Way Books for taking on and supporting this collection; to Paula Bohince, Monica Ferrell, Alexandra Socarides, and Craig Morgan Teicher for invaluable feedback on drafts of the collection in manuscript; to my parents, for reading aloud to my siblings and me well into my teens; and to Robert Farnsworth and Lisa Russ Spaar *ad infinitum.* Finally, my thanks to and for Martha Kelly, whose balance of exuberance for and insight into these poems is perfection.

Gabriel Fried is an editor and poet. He is the author of *Making the New Lamb Take*, which was named a best poetry book of 2007 by *Foreword* magazine and the *St. Louis Post-Dispatch*, and the editor of an anthology, *Heart of the Order: Baseball Poems*. He lives in Columbia, Missouri.

Publication of this book was made possible by grants and donations. We are also grateful to those individuals who participated in our 2016 Build a Book Program. They are:

Anonymous (8), Evan Archer, Sally Ball, Jan Bender-Zanoni, Zeke Berman, Kristina Bicher, Carol Blum, Lee Briccetti, Deirdre Brill, Anthony Cappo, Carla & Steven Carlson, Maxwell Dana, Machi Davis, Monica Ferrell, Martha Webster & Robert Fuentes, Dorothy Goldman, Lauri Grossman, Steven Haas, Mary Heilner, Henry Israeli, Christopher Kempf, David Lee, Jen Levitt, Howard Levy, Owen Lewis, Paul Lisicky, Katie Longofono, Cynthia Lowen, Louise Mathias, Nathan McClain, Gregory McDonald, Britt Melewski, Kamilah Aisha Moon, Carolyn Murdoch, Tracey Orick, Zachary Pace, Gregory Pardlo, Allyson Paty, Marcia & Chris Pelletiere, Eileen Pollack, Barbara Preminger, Kevin Prufer, Peter & Jill Schireson, Roni & Richard Schotter, Soraya Shalforoosh, Peggy Shinner, James Snyder & Krista Fragos, Megan Staffel, Marjorie & Lew Tesser, Susan Walton, Calvin Wei, Abigail Wender, Allison Benis White, and Monica Youn.